BULLIES
IN LOVE

Reviews

"How can one voice be so raw and so refined? How can a poet so fiercely female speak more universally than those who deny our differences? The electrifying paradoxes of art and life snap from every page here as Reiter names the driving forces of her life—*our* lives."
—**Nancy White**, administrator of The Word Works Washington Prize, author of *Detour* (Tamarack Editions, 2010).

"Bitter, tender, contained, full of pain and hilarity, this fiercely intelligent collection begins with one of the most beautiful poems I have ever read. 'Inconsolable joy,' Reiter writes to her newborn son. 'Motherless, I mother.' Within this grace all questions resolve: 'Each glinting wavelet a day of my history,/washing my hands as I lose it.' The history to be known and released includes childhood abuse, and cruelties both familial and social...In these poems, theology becomes concrete and passionate."
—**Ruth Thompson**, author of *Woman with Crows* (Saddle Road Press, 2013), A Room of Her Own Foundation "To the Lighthouse" Prize Finalist.

"Jendi Reiter's astute observations of the complex nature of love reveal not only its beauty but also its damning consequences. From the child to the adult, the home to the wider world, this collection of affirming yet disturbing tight-knit poetry in various forms kaleidoscopes vivid images, framing the struggle to free oneself from parental and societal expectations from start to finish. These poems span the coming-of-age search for self-respect and love; the ideologies of marketing and religion; teachers' censorship of children's literature; and political crimes against sexual minorities."
—**Suzanne Covich**, child rights activist and educator, author of *When We Remember They Call Us Liars* (Fremantle Press, 2012).

"Lyric, narrative, prose poem...in all her work Jendi Reiter is constantly innovating, injecting her lines with fresh, sharp language and taut, piercing images which yes, surprise, exhilarate, and delight, but also force the reader to rethink their relationships to social forces. The nature of love and desire are here, but so are family, faith, the body, the natural world, pop culture...even a few stray cats. Jendi explores these as both priestess and stand-up comedian, deploying reverence and humor (sometimes at the same time), and gazing upon whimsy and atrocity with equal scrutiny."
—**Charlie Bondhus**, author of *All the Heat We Could Carry* (Main Street Rag, 2013), 2014 Thom Gunn Award for Gay Poetry.

"Beyond her impressive verbal pyrotechnics, there's an invigorating way of making unexpected connections, as in this from one of my favorite poems, 'What Dora Said to Agnes': 'When a man undresses a woman/ he is unfolding a letter/he expected would be addressed to him…' and in the same poem: 'When a woman undresses a man/she is promising to wash him,/she is offering the hand that will close his eyes.' Reiter's uncommon insights into love, partnering, sorrow, death and new ways of living, together and apart, will inspire and comfort the fellow traveler, the reader, you."
—**Robert McDowell**, author of *Poetry as Spiritual Practice* and *The World Next to This One*; www.robertmcdowell.net.

"In her remarkable collection of poems, *Bullies In Love*, Jendi Reiter has created a complex odditorium of characters with unique and often disturbing voices: poems peopled with bullies, the disenfranchised, monsters, prostitutes, criminals, the abused and forgotten, all searching for meaning, for faith and love in a postmodern, often cynical world."
—**Pamela Uschuk**, author of *Crazy Love*, 2010 American Book Award Winner, and *Blood Flower* (Wings Press).

Winner of the
Little Red Tree International Poetry Prize

BULLIES
IN LOVE

JENDI REITER

FIRST EDITION

Little Red Tree Publishing, LLC,
635 Ocean Avenue, New London, CT 06320

Layout and Cover Design: Michael Linnard
Text in Minion Pro, Trajan Pro and Arial.

First Edition, 2015, manufactured in USA
1 2 3 4 5 6 7 8 9 10 LSI 20 19 18 17 16 15

All previous publication credits of a number of poems in this collection are listed at the back of this book [p 97].

In poem "third day" [p 36], the lines in italics are adapted, with kind permission, from the April 11, 2010 Associated Press story, "Even in death, African gays are still abused."

Front cover photograph is by Toni Pepe. Also photographs on pages: i, 1, 21, 45, 69, 95, and 105 [with short biography].

Photograph of Jendi Reiter, on back cover and page 207, by Ed Judice.

Library of Congress Cataloging-in-Publication Data

Reiter, Jendi
  Bullies in Love / Jendi Reiter. -- 1st ed.
    p. cm.
  Includes index
  ISBN 978-1-935656-36-4 (pbk. : alk. paper)
  I. Title.
  PS3612.A58565S77 2015
  811'.6--dc23
                                2015012871

Little Red Tree Publishing LLC
635 Ocean Avenue,
New London Connecticut 06320
www.littleredtree.com

CONTENTS

ACKNOWLEDGEMENTS

Thanks to the Massachusetts Cultural Council for supporting the writing of this book with an Artists' Grant for Poetry in 2010. Dan Blask at the MCC also connected me with fellow grant recipient Toni Pepe, whose fine art photography graces these pages.

A number of these poems were written for the "30 Poems in November" 2010, 2011, and 2014 fundraisers for the Center for New Americans, a nonprofit in Northampton, MA that offers adult literacy programs and assistance for immigrant families. Support their work at www.cnam.org.

Ellen LaFleche, who is peerless as both a poet and a friend, helped me revise this manuscript and identify its main themes. Her award-winning chapbooks include *Workers' Rites* (The Poet's Press, 2011), selected for the Providence Athenaeum's Philbrick Poetry Prize by former U.S. Poet Laureate Dana Gioia: www.poetspress.org/catalog.shtml#lafleche

Finally, thanks to my family for providing love, inspiration, and amusement. My husband, Adam Cohen, came up with the most original premises for the poems in this book; for example, the idea that "Love is a violent town in Texas" and the poem title "Poem Written on the Side of a Cow," and the weird AP News story that inspired "Robot Deer Shot 1,000 Times." He has also written the definitive parodies of my work, which he is forbidden to share with anyone. My mom-of-choice, Roberta Pato, is my role model for healing from trauma with hopefulness and gratitude. My beautiful son, Shane Steven Cohen, born in 2012, teaches me how to write books with happy endings.

Section I

Lord of the Storm

Here is the ocean I promised you
salting your forehead with my fingertips.

Inconsolable joy.
Motherless, I mother.

Brown foam sucks the sand from under my toes,
digging a hollow shaped like my standing.

Six-weeks boy, swaddled blue as Cape waters,
your cries scouring my heart.

Down the driftwood stairs, down to the eroded coast,
carrying you, the first trust in my arms.

You came from a longer sea,
a more constant sun.

Neither of us belong to time,
un-homed from the country of sleep.

I'd thought waking for you would be no harder
than my old midnight pattern of terrors.

Three a.m. in the mildewed sunroom,
no one breathing but us and the dark waters.

All the silences wore off at once.
My ghosts became baby birds pleading not to starve.

Today's ocean has hush enough
to spread spangled to the pearly horizon.

Each glinting wavelet a day of my history,
washing my hands as I lose it.

Your shrimp-pink fingers curl at my neck.
You open stone-blue eyes to summer's glare.

You have no name for yourself or mother
or drowning or birth, so I will tell you:

That solid shape rocking on the distant current
could be a boat where a friend lies sleeping

as bravely as we will sleep tonight,
a man who knows where he comes from and where he is going.

I Wish I Were in Love Again

When Sinatra sings,
I wish I were in love again,
I imagine Love is the name
of a violent town in Texas
where the one stoplight
took a bullet long ago,
dusting the dry street with ruby glass.

Where the sheriff,
big-bellied as Cupid,
didn't see the evidence
of the split rope, the double-smudged lipstick,
the blacksnake-cold gun under the belt.

Sinatra's voice pours the golden
whiskey of nostalgia to shimmer
over the icy rocks, like the foothills
outside Love where nothing
lives but tumbleweeds and chicken thieves.
He misses the spat of cat and cur,
the flying fur, the sparks
that burned down Love's one church
when the preacher's daughter
fell asleep smoking.

Lucky in Love
is the man who didn't miss the train
in or out of town.

Love is a Many-Splendored Thing,
the mayor says,
hoping to attract
a branch of the Houston bank,
a brassworks factory or even a circus
to settle in Love,
create jobs for the men
and scarcer women who lie

in saloon alleys all night clutching
souvenirs of Love to their hearts:
a postcard, a clump of red dirt.
Who wouldn't want such a loyal workforce?

Love is just around the corner,
if you've got a first-class horse.

City-trippers in the mood
for the blackened eyes
Sinatra sighs for
take the spur line to Love
en route to Laredo or Dallas.
Fanning themselves with transfer tickets,
the ladies breathe,
I've never been in Love before,
mistaking the crash of plates
for an emphatic whorehouse piano.

The general store hawks banjos
with one string, plasters for the knees
of old folks who fall in Love too easily,
and of course, bullets.
If you break a hip in Love
you know what happens.

Despite the weather,
Love's no place to retire.
The all-you-can-eat buffet closes at five.
When the moon climbs the sky again
like a drunk husband going upstairs,
the city ladies take their seats
in the second-class carriage,
each with a purple bloom
aching under her blouse, or against her cheek.
It won't fade for days.
It's almost like being in Love.

The Scientist Tells His Mother About the Moon

She read in his paper that the moon's one face
stares, at all points in its orbit,
at the ocean-swaddled globe.
Its other face, she
read also, leans into the dark
like a housebound child
fixated on the busy night's
thousand windows.
It's because that gravity
(he wrote) peculiar to themselves
is just the strength
to trap the moon before she falls
upon her fat-cheeked planet, at last
connected by more
than the umbilical tides —
but also just the strength
to stop her dancing
away in a drunken, widening reel,
scattering stars like baby teeth.

712

because i could not stop for death
i blew my whistle
death said hey baby
you're my old lady
sixteen with a learner's permit
and those shoes make you look legal

because i got tired of spraying
death in the eyes
watching him
thrash around on the floor like a white guy
trying to breakdance
i let him buy me that
drink with the cherry parasol
and didn't take it to the lab first
in my itsy-bitsy vodkatini post-bikini
death said hey baby
what's your sign
hoping i'd say yield
i said
a cloud no bigger than a man's hand

because i fisted my car keys like norman
bates' knife in the shower
parked under the neon
dummy in the front seat
in my bed by midnight
except the drummer was still tingle-tang-banging
when the last bus pulled away in the rain
and oh hell i was ready
to spread my legs like a hand
of aces just once
death said hey baby
and i put my chips on red
and i put my chips on black

Trigger Warning for Fur

I was in love with grandmother's cat.
Before him Big Bird, my prince but not a good one,
stiff and stuffed. Four years old.
Grandfather's heart stopped in the street.
Sidney was white with orange spots and brass-bright eyes.
Cushions pink and plush couldn't be touched
under zippered plastic.
Later I grew hair on my thighs.
The doctor asked mother how many sandwiches I ate.
Wrong number, the ambulance came too late.
Sidney was the only male in the house.
I wore a red T-shirt with his name but they spelled
it wrong with two Y's and the cat decal too
a sour flat-faced Persian.
Later I grew breasts.
Mother came home every night to be comforted
and aunt slept alone in peachy sheets
scattered with clips and pins.
The doctor recommended electricity for my face.
A needle in each hair.
Grandmother fed them tuna behind the dumpster
and when she died, aunt did it.
Later I bled.
Mother said never accept
an open can of soda from a boy.
Sidney's belly fur grew long and swayed.
We stopped eating at the same time.
Rubbed my face against his soft hot stomach
till my eyes went red.
I kept doing it.
The doctor said you couldn't expect strays to live long.
Tumors the size of kittens.
When they cut him open I found out he'd been a girl.

The Name-Stone

(Revelation 2:17)

I will give you a stone
with a secret under it.

As children in the Galilee
wrote friendship's names on both ends
of such a shard, and broke it
and went away, each to his own desert.

Dirt-born,
nothing to give one another
but a ragged edge
that, fit
to its companion, meant love.

Where do the gouged letters lie,
in temple midden or the royal road's thorns?
What hands crushed the clay?

I will give you a piece
of unmarked earth.

Not the name
your mother pressed onto your lips
to seal the scroll of her sorrows.

Not the name
your father spilled
like an ox-dragged harrow,
a plow with no sower.

They only know the name
that decoy, death,
reared above the spot
where you left this ground.

Granite praises granite,
butchers weep
over the marble lamb,
speak both parts
of the absolving script.

But I will give you a riven rock
to drink from its flood heart,
the rock I broke myself
to fit you.

Poem With Nothing Before 1972

You were so young and modern
with your name like a fold-out corduroy sofa,
with your name like the glamour detective,
Mrs. Hart-to-Hart, with your name
so popular you spit it out
under the back row desks, stuck
it and left it in fossilized Dubble Bubble,
because you never could tell,
in that echo of alphabets and subtraction,
if you were the one called on.

You were so new and plastic
that you cried when Marlena was strangled
the first time,
on Days of Our Lives.
She was the heroine, which meant her eyes brimmed
with unselfish secrets, glistening in the 2 PM fadeout.
Only you knew what kept her from her lover
while your parents fried chicken livers and argued.
The next day, like so many
stories you were told, it never happened.
It was her twin, like her a therapist,
who laid down her feathered honey
princess hair on death's couch to tease you.
Last time you saw her, you were on jury duty
twenty years of hourglasses later,
and she was possessed by the devil.

You were so bright and straight-edged
you still hoped to slip through the rules
like a skate blade on a stiff white boot.
For your mother's rule against artificial colors,
you snuck only the brown M&Ms.
For her rule against dirt, your hair was vacuumed
till you stopped building sandcastles.
You collected bricks instead.
For her rule against watching, you didn't know

anything about the trash compactor,
not feeding after midnight, why they were here.
The Empire may have struck back
but you wouldn't, always at the bottom
of the wading pool, because of the rule of turning
the other cheek (your own).
But you sang Maxwell's Silver Hammer
whether there was music or not.

Bullies in Love

Wouldn't it be nice to believe all hate is desire,
the bullet that wings the bird
wanting to be a bird?
Believe, if little dead boys can
hold their dear opinions in the ground,
that the fist is only a heart
stunned by too much muscle?
Because then you would still be visible,
chosen as carefully for destruction
as the cities of the plain
or the shy girl in a vampire novel,
the girl who is all elbows and sorrow
and stands outside at weddings.
The truth is, most hatred is different from really rough sex,
neither masked for the sizzle of mystery
nor screaming the name of the defeated, its own.
Not thinking is its flavor.
Deafness, its spice.
But believe, because you are not yet twenty-one
and drowning, not yet lying down at seventeen
beneath the homecoming train, not yet a choking thirteen
hung from your mother's garage ceiling,
because you are still at home on prom night
watching the Discovery Channel, you will be convinced
that the zebras, by now, must be aware of the cameras
and that the one who tumbles beneath the lion's
rank delicious weight is choosing
something like the mating that escaped you.

Depression Is My Happy Place

that lake waits anytime
for me to slip
under its threaded green hush
i don't need summer or parking
to arrive
where my hurtling family
is already one less

depression is easy to get to
even on holidays
the standards are lower than church
or kindergarten
you can run with scissors there
but you probably won't bother

it's my tight light box
where i turn back the sun
to a pale hum

i don't need fattening pills
or fermented dizzy bottles
i can spin it on my own
straw into lead
because a lead house
never blows down or burns

side effects of depression may include
eating more or less
than people in magazines
sleeping more or less
by yourself
sudden loss of interest
in what your mother thinks

it's my soft dust pillow
under the boxspring where grandma money
refuses the bankers' conjurations

of brown fields into winking green numbers
racing round the globe
like a tornado-spun house

it's my black screen
i won't trade

there may be a cost-saving generic
alternative to depression
ask your doctor about marriage
smiling often and wearing a good suit
may cause people to leave you alone
did you know that your natural skin tone
adds a layer of protection at no extra charge
(some restrictions may apply)

depression is not recommended
for unattractive women

touching story

not the turn to gold but touch he
wanted most, no object that
flesh of his
supper gelled to shining
ore lumps when he bit, that sepals
stiffened on the rose
like nipples bared to frost. not
the lark that lasted but the scar
its moneyed weight peeled
down the tree. not the trophy
hound, that sudden andiron
dropped from his lap,
but the fox, stinking, invisible,
unchased.
                   myth to asses' ears,
no nodding velveted clefts
named his errata, not a page
or armed barber kissed the riverbed
to scandalize the reeds
into singing true. and when his daughter,
as he'd tell it, sprang
into his transmuting arms, and after,
there was no god to take the hardening gift away.

What Dora Said to Agnes

I have begun to think I was not fit to be a wife.
—David Copperfield, *Chapter 53*

When a man falls in love with a woman in a painting,
they call it philosophy.
When a woman falls asleep with a book under her pillow,
they call it loneliness.
When a man brings a woman home from the massage parlor,
when he buys the teen runaway a donut
that she eats greedily,
shivering angry in her brother's outgrown sweater,
when on the yellowed thousandth page of a novel
the girl who was too beautiful for her neighbors
dies fully clothed in the preacher's arms,
it is not the same as when a woman imagines
gently removing Sherlock Holmes' tweed cape and hat,
coaxing Frankenstein down from the ice cliffs
with a cup of warm milk,
it is said to have nothing in common with jailhouse weddings,
the women who write of love to famous killers,
pushing themselves up against police sawhorses
as the televised glare kisses their lipstick
at the stuttering electric stroke of midnight.
When a man undresses a woman
he is unfolding a letter
he expected would be addressed to him,
when he reads it whatever memories
he brought to it he will take away again.
When a woman undresses a man
she is promising to wash him,
she is offering the hand that will close his eyes.

The Deer Problem

for Hannah

A gray-white streak across the forest trail,
chased by a burst of dogs.

Uneven mouth-holes in the soil by the white lace fence.
Bad taste didn't save the daffodils.

All year round I slept with my window locked,
afraid the yipping thing would steal me.

The deer were moving in too close, my parents said,
nibbling the gardens we cut out of the woods.

Because our town was small, we had bears delivered
from city yards where they'd torn through the garbage.

They had no natural predators, there were too many
tawny heads leaning over back fences, munching flowers.

A bear pawed through pots, upstairs we thought
the noise was my father, coming home to eat without talking.

They were lazy too, preferring trash to venison,
teaching their bumbling cubs to drop melon rinds in the driveway.

Men arrived in unmarked trucks.
We were told to clear the area for that day.

They were delivering crates of wolves.
They hadn't asked permission from anyone we knew.

Our daffodils flourished like five-star generals.
We came inside with our games before dark.

I saw the brown dog and the black dog,
leashes trailing, pursue the blur of wolf.

I saw but I don't know if I saw
a lost loner picked off or a new pack joining.

Section II

Period Piece

I'm on the poetry rag
my womb can't hold a job
it spits out bar napkins of inspiration
streaks of drunken grand plans
like Bukowski's wine-stained typescripts
I've got my Sunday visitor
and it's not a Catholic magazine
though nuns must synchronize like periodicals
black and white and red all over
I'm scratching my mosquito bite
as Lizzie Borden called the spot
on her trial skirt
because ladybusiness is murder
I'm painting the town
I've got company
Aunt Flo's camped on my horsehair sofa
playing Old Maid with a deck of diamonds
and knitting tube socks for soldiers
the redcoats are coming
but don't be afraid
of me riding the white horse
out where the cattle stampede
it's just that time of the month when I like
my steak with a little ketchup

Trigger Warning for Sailors

Beckoned, drunk, by a mermaid's
permanent stain, I shrank
from the needle's blue.
I might have to change
my face someday,
turn my voyage inside-out,
a thief reversing his coat in the crowd.

A rare risk, I know.
More likely I'll slip
under the unmarked green ocean
stitched in a linen sack.
No bunkmate to joke
that I wore my bones on my sleeve.

They all look the same, at sea,
skulls winking on sail-hoisting shoulders,
blue roses creeping up bowed legs,
an easy girl on every arm
copied from flash.

What else remains—Names?
Anchors? The portside artist,
her needle restless as a watch's
second hand, pushed the Mom heart:
Every man had a mother.
But a trash bin was my cradle,
and I'm not alone
among those who take to the sea.

I've shared my hammock with men
of greater faith, who carved the blue memory
of hometown loves on their backs.
Through storms, we've swung in a dark
so complete I couldn't read
the log of their shipwrecks.

Our wake draws a line
of minutes to the dock.
I'll drink the night with friends,
wake up talked into angels
penned for life on my chest.
Remember, body,
the water undoes us at last.

Poem Written on the Side of a Cow

Let me tell you, dying
is just my way of being useful,
after the good years of milking and the green
path you led me down, soil yielding as cake;
all over now, my brute, my honey-
handed farmer.

Remember when the scent of my slow breath
contained a meadow, and you owned the meadow.
Remember when you wouldn't let the flies settle,
once, on my skin.

It's an awkward transition that leaves me
throatless, hung from my heels like a trapeze artist.
Some woman will look better in my skin,
proud as a raven in black leather.
My fat turned to plastic—o magic
America—a motorcycle's hull.
Rewarded hounds chew on my hooves.
Who could argue
with a dog's happiness?

So press the last drops from me
with the old, mechanical suckling.
Lead me down the hillside to stare
once more at the fence, my white church,
my home of bounded beliefs.
There will be meat for weary fathers,
boots for their feet. All that I promised.

I was furniture, a toothless piano,
by the time the truck came to spare me.
Just remember the snow, like worn fleece,
that tried to blanket your ears
from the rumble of butchers' wheels.
Remember how you gave the children
their glasses of milk, of still-warm milk,
then locked the door.

Resistance

Cheek against the woodgrain O forgive
   (gray perfume of wax and rain)
this need of man strength of honor's fist
   (how like a mouse into the crushed cushions)
against the rape the spit and tearing
   (I brought my pain. The small dry seeds.)
and why not stand in sun though we stand on nothing
   (sage incense of ash of libraries)
begrudge me not protection till your terrible rescue
   (everything that breathes here is already burnt)

Knees against the leather I feel the arms
   (how soon the boot blinds the battered clay)
falling and falling like axes
   (across your face is mine)
little rats the flesh worries
   (the brain waits for those other cold teeth)
who would not raise the Barabbas hand
   (seeing himself raised)

Still against the stone the silence bells
   (under the dress darkness under the soles smoke)
something passes not time but its longer shadow
   (behold the same sky prisoner torturer)
where was he night nailed to day between them
   (in the tomb in the middle of time)
terrible it passes will we fear him
   (stronger than the evil stones)

Trigger Warning *Pour Homme*

L'Air du Temps
was the secret name of all perfume,
drained vial stoppered with paired doves
slowing the last wisps of scent's escape.
Ingredients, labels, are just recipes
read by a child without a mouth.
They don't re-animate the days
of scalloped handkerchiefs and gloves in a cedar drawer
where my mother stashed untouchable rings.

Le De Givenchy
lay in my underwear,
hip flask suffusing my cotton-strap, flat-chest tees
with crushed Italian violets, musk of taxicabs and stilettos.
My mother's one glamour photo, hair pinned high
as she never wore it, ascended over my dresser
where the plastic girl on the box lid spun in place
like the dancer she would have been.

Old Spice
came in a sample mailer to our house of ladies,
a misdirected cowboy trailing the heavy
sweetness of deep voices in close-packed rooms.
I dripped it on my paper doll men
to make them smell like lovers,
at the age when my friends were starting
to drink the soda breath of boys.

Obsession
was a scent for my eyes,
only reaching me from billboards,
black and white its ceaseless two-note
mating call.

Estée Lauder's Beautiful
tried too hard to sell its charms,
like the girl who wore emerald lamé to the prom

where I wore a Puerto Rican wedding dress.
Of the bottle, the flavor, nothing sticks but the pinkness
of the advertised woman and child, their flower crowns and tulle
in the sun of the meadow of their embrace.
My mother didn't wear it for long.

Revlon Unforgettable
crooned in city shades of Nat King Cole,
brass and lipstick red the skyscraper bottle.
My wrists smelled like a midtown hotel
suite I shared with another winning college girl
for the fashion magazine breakfast.
I smelled loud as a phone, inky as Cindy Crawford's
proud imperfect mole.
My mother coughed when she met me at the airport.
That summer, my twenty-first,
she'd become allergic to all perfume.

Safe Word

Yesterday you got married and today you write about being beaten
    like a shield, hammered pleasure, surrendered gold.

If I were beaten it would be like an egg.

That is why I avoid it.

I avoid it because I have no father.

I avoid it in a dish of money.

There is only one cock between us and
    it makes me sad as tissue paper.

Yesterday you were not ironic among the roses
    man to man saying love was solid
    as Sparta's marble bones.

Today who watches you hang in the harness
    groan in the traces
    split from your skin like a shot crow?

Love, but not only him.

If I said husband it would mean padlock.

It would mean camouflage of two foxes under snow.

Two baby foxes under the unbroken glide of the bird's shadow.

I am lonely finding my language
    only understood by the boring half of the world,
    the half that cries when their sons are beaten.

Sweet guilty, you, Pièta slinking from Mary's
    lap to the scourge again.

Excuse me, I said to the lion.

Thumbs down on the third date.

If there was a word that made treaty with teeth
        that suspended the whip's blood in the air like roses
        that unfurled soft tongues from the gladiator's spear
what a nice world for poets and little girls.

I was never not guilty but I was always innocent,
        if innocence means wearing too many flowers.

Rubber Poem

A more famous poet's best friend once said
if you don't risk sentimentality in a poem why bother.
Sentimentality is what we call feelings
that the writer is wholly inside of, but no one else is.
In that sense it's the safest poetry act, no risk of transmission.
Videos of masturbation will always get more clicks than poetry
about the world wars or Midwestern childhood or discovering radium
or even love,
which suggests that sentimentality is unfairly maligned.
It's only a quarter
to peep through the glory hole of the poem
at the man wincing and sighing at the feeling of himself,
and we do, though the moves are so generic
he could be rocking to earbud music, or taking a burning piss
because he went bare the last time, what a mistake.
Sentiment-discordant couples, now that's a risk.
Unlike what the health pamphlets tell you,
it's usually the negative who converts the positive.
After enough unprotected encounters
the writer becomes immune to roses,
may go blind to the moon, contract
every stanza with ironic ampersands.
This poem is not like that.
It feels like real skin.
There's a space at the tip to catch your teardrops.
If used correctly, the risk of reading this poem is lower
than what you did last night. Go ahead, now,
no one is watching.

Polish Joke

This circus has been in our family
forty years, no,
round it up to a hundred—
from the days of us bundled and stowed
out of the old country faster than horses,
lucky as a round number,
one skinny papa with two zero eyes.
You wouldn't have believed to look at us
that we were carrying a circus.
Back then, it was just fleas.

But what gets you across the ocean
except a conjurer who pulls
scarves of red battles, blue hills and yellow butter
out of his memory hat
for weeks in the seasick dark?
Who charms fat rabbits
out of an empty cupboard
except a dame hard enough
to tango with pythons
and disappear a sword down her throat?

Later, when we had enough eggs to juggle,
we added some new members
you might recognize:

The girl who jumps from high places,
that versatile girl
who is not really sawed in half,
who is not really rising asleep from her bed
snagged on invisible wires.
The bickering family with flapping shoes
and greasepaint smiles red as borscht,
honking up in their tiny car
through the middle of somebody else's ballet,
laughter sticking to them like flypaper.
The young fellow with eyes black as magnets

who combs out golden manes,
leads tawny bodies through caged tricks,
but makes the anxious ladies wet their handkerchiefs
by sticking his head for a moment
in the whipped animal's jaws.

Our greatest addition was the strongman:
Even forty years,
no, call it a hundred
since he's been gone,
his sausage-armed sons
and their sons after them
are still pounding that mallet
against the target at their feet,
sweating to make that same bell ring
loud enough to shatter
the old man's perfect score.

When Should You Tell Your Children About Satan?

First they took away the goats, then the pictures of goats.
When the little ones cried, our teachers
said we'd left the gate open for them to wander,
and then no one said anything.
The three gruffs became lambs
in the blue and yellow drawings in our new books,
and the troll smiled at their softness
with no red ink teeth in sight.

The stars on our papers were the right way up
and turned to F's if we drew circles around them.
In the cafeteria, there was no mustard
in our hard-boiled eggs, and the cake
was white as a good princess's heart.
Biology posters stopped at the neck.
Our teachers wouldn't tolerate the pirate flag
skull-face jawing at them, not even for science.

They were very kind to us. We felt fine
without noodles in our alphabet soup,
skipping number six and thirteen
when we counted off who was It.
The kids who didn't get their turn
under the new system—let's call them Lucy and Nick,
only we couldn't, because those names weren't allowed—
weren't crying. They went to play someplace else.
We heard the screech of the swing set,
the happy thumps of a rubber ball.
Anyway we had to stop calling them "kids"
because that's what a goat is, to start with.
When the mother left her seven little ones
at home in the storybook
and the wolf came, the way our teachers told it
no one was really there, no one got eaten.

third day

In memory of Madieye Diallo, May 2, 2009, Dakar, Senegal.

neighbor   *the shaky image*
neighbor *wind blew*
  fine gray dirt   too shallow
neighbor   *the dirt*
  they shoveled   another man believed
it was because of the wedding
it was because of the disease
watched *from behind the wall*
neighbor the hole unfilled
with a rope around its feet
        it was him
        its torso his feet
because a man fed a man
                dragged
        it away   spit on
        it   dumped
wedding cake and wine
because he appeared in the photograph
                people were rejoicing
                another man believed
he had no medicine
he had it but he could not take it
                24 hours
he had it but he could not reach it
                or face decapitation
the hospital had a wing
for his disease
the family had no mouth
                he is not here
                he is not here
                there are no homosexuals here
because the poor you have always
distracted with shined pots and wrung-neck birds
because hands need a hole

in Senegal's newspapers and magazines
in the time of the prophet
two men were taken to a mountaintop
if they didn't die when they hit the ground
if they were found together
            in cemeteries
            in a rented banquet hall
            in an established democracy
because barefoot because burning
            another man believed
            to be gay
neighbor if the *trash passes*
the body cannot lie
if it passes *his sons*
  on the side of the road
in a sheet white black the body
  before the family could bathe
him chased from the temple *using their own*
        hands to dig
trash cannot lie with the dead
neighbor the good dead

> *"People were rejoicing," he says.*
> *"They dragged him past me and his*
> *body left tracks in the sand. Like a*
> *car passing through snow."*

The lines in italics are adapted, with kind permission, from the April 11, 2010 Associated Press story, "Even in death, African gays are still abused."

World's Fattest Cat Has World's Fattest Kittens

—Tabloid headline

A man walks into a bar and that's
how I meet my father. Thirty years' prelude
to a first date, in the amber mood
of brass and cognac, philosophic chat
spins the barstool back and I could be my mother
making us something intimate and undefined,
making someone you would leave behind.
My job-interview smile like butter
over the Riviera snaps of your daughters,
an alternate normalcy unreeled
by their tan arms, nothing concealed
behind your soft, proud chest but beach and blue waters.
But my awkward sister, dark-eyed—can't you find
her moon-round face in yours, and yours in mine?

Tapas and wine, and God to take his turn
building the polite fortress of conversation;
two ex-Jews still wedded to disputation
and self-pity. The theatre crowd, as unconcerned
as you with tabloid reunions, disperses
into Manhattan's blue lure. I say Jesus ended
life for our trespasses, but you're offended
at this old, barbarous economy of verses.
You glow with gurus, out-of-body flight
and sinless man—convenient to believe
the soul can shed the seeds the body leaves.
And I, lacking the charity not to hate your
smooth life apart from us—who am I to spite
the last lawyer who has faith in human nature?

Dumb girl, ludicrous heredity
making me hang on your kisses like a teen,
then ask, like the boy-father to the child unseen,
who is this one, this virtual life, to me?
True father, tell me now, don't we both nurse
our entitlements like a spitting-image son,

me judging life's gift by how it was begun,
you grasping after apples with no curse?
Atonement's just about dousing a blaze
someone else started. Till then, the wheel and snare
of karmic alleles conspires down the years
to put our eyes in an accusing face.
Tabloids and Genesis agree on that:
fat kittens must have come from fatter cats.

Outside Faces

"It's the happiest place on earth,"
says a girl entering "Faces",
the downtown shop that sells monkey masks
and leggings in her slender size and magnets
with jokes about PMS and beer.
Since that's the only line I catch
as she and her boyfriend, or maybe just a friend,
pass me exiting the glass double doors,
I don't know if she means where she's going
or where she's just left, or some other place
such as Disney World or a Samoan village
she's studying in her Smith College seminar,
a roomful of girls in wool scarves softly debating
how it would feel to live together
under a palm-frond roof, feeding mangoes
to each other's babies, with no more term papers.

At the Coca-Cola museum, on our wedding anniversary,
we watched a cartoon called "The Happiness Factory",
the upshot being that soda pop eases heartbreak
for baby monsters who fall in love with dandelions.
They didn't mention cocaine,
an important component of happiness
for Freud, who might have said the womb
was the place the girl was talking about,
whether or not she realized it.
It's easier to misconstrue that oceanic feeling
when you look good in a bikini.

If she knew the happiest place on earth
was a beach, a library cozy with mildew and steam heat,
between velvet skirts
on the 50-cent carousel at the Hospice Shop,
would it be smart to go there,
since by definition
no place later in all
her years after twenty could compare?

Maybe on a warm October Thursday night
happiness lay in the street where I exited,
the snow melted and the power lines patched
and a few stores lit again for anyone
with spare change enough for pizza or rubber boots
and a postcard from the Art-O-Mat.

Lost Cat

after Amy Hwang, New Yorker Sept. 19, 2011

A cat in a turtleneck regards a poster of himself,
thinking, *I'm not lost,*
I moved on to better things.

This is a New Yorker cartoon,
so the cat has probably been in therapy
where he learned to reframe his four-legged past
like an ex-wife snipping one face from her photos.

We can assume he holds the correct views.
Republicans rarely wear turtlenecks.

Little girls have been known to lose their faith
when their cat runs away.
Some break down glimpsing the garbage truck
that maybe crushed the love from their limp friend,
God muscling the wheel
in the high cab, rolling on.

For others it's the priest or aunt
fortressed in starched lace,
duty-bound to insist
there's no pet heaven.

No wonder the cat put on shoes.
What if he wanted to walk into a bar?
What if he needed a new punchline
at the Pearly Gates?

The devils in funny-hell are just working stiffs.
One cat more or less in the inbox
is nothing to them.
They pass eternity one panel at a time
with sarcastic remarks,
like aunts only with beards and no clothes.

A game can be lost, and a key,
a race and a chance.
What was once called *maidenhead*.
The point of a joke.

The priests and the aunts plaster up
this label though they know exactly
where those so-called are headed:
worse than a hump of desert island
with a desperate man and one coconut palm.
Someplace not funny at all.

Do you know Jesus?
If found, call.

The girl in the turtleneck
in the city doesn't believe
she's going to the same heaven
as those subscribers. She is lost
like a phone call,
a signal, virginity, the cat
who, she still hopes,
missed her too.

Possession

I collect packets of soup noodles. The last pages of books from the prison library. I am a collector of others' facial expressions. If you've found it hard to move your eyebrows lately, that was probably me. I collect the different colors the day appears in. Soup noodles crackle. There are many colors that are called gray. Dawn light and potato soup and regulation wool socks. I would collect them all, except I have nowhere to store the soup. Cellophane wrappers crackle as if something more was in them than you could see through. Fire and footsteps. Even in here there are hobbies I have no time for. I do not collect rats. They have no numbers. Unlike us. Every rat is the same number, meaning, more than you can see. Rats do not have the patience to collect soup noodles. That is why they will temporarily be your friend, again and again. Rats shrink from the sound of crackling, like a teenage boy forced to read a nineteenth-century novel of manners. The Victorians were so unsure of themselves that they collected the hair of the dead. Wove it into fetishes of gray flower brooches. Because they didn't know anymore whether the soul had another place to go home to. Rapping and tapping, the dead return to turn out their pocket litter, to prove themselves by the ticket stubs and cigarette butts their unique past collected. Proving they are made of paper and ash. Like the clipboard woman sent by the state to ask me to circle how I am feeling today. I feel like the number 4. She does not want any soup noodles. I have found that most people, when they hear the sound of crackling, remember their dream of being followed through a dark wood.

Section III

What Does It Mean When You Dream of the Ocean?

Cthulhu's got issues with his mother.
Ten thousand years old and he still wets the couch.
He could always eat the doctor,
snap like a skinny lobster leg
in his octopus beak, but frankly,
he's too bored to find another.
How he misses the cold black deep, the misshapen towers,
the endless waiting, half-asleep
among slow and nameless things.
Now words clog his gullet like broken clamshells
and every sightline has an edge.

He picks up a crayon,
a rake from the sand tray,
and drawing a trail
of slime on the Chinese carpet,
describes the Black Goat of the Woods.

Very interesting.
It must stand for something else.
R'lyeh wgah'nagl fhtagn,
Cthulhu explains. The doctor writes
DSM-5 297.1, 301.7.

He waits for the spell of her symbols
to send a blinding color through the window,
the anti-white, prism of unseeable shades.
His suckers stick to the leatherette.
Eons ago some creature must have pushed him
out of her cave into a greater one,
but what matters memory?
These human bugs, these prawns,
trace their inch-long lives in sand,
look down to the scribble for reasons,
blind to the stars.

Risperidone 2 mg/d.

Cthulhu wakes
at 4 AM from the dream of a woman
in a black bustle, a pin at her neck,
telling her child he's too ugly to go outside
their wooden house whose steps tumble down to the docks.
Copper and salt singe the air.
The sheets are wet and he is hungry.

not with the old leaven

butch girl half face painted   towels the pink off her cheek
glassy tear tacked to her eye   hard as man hands   reaching up
to scrape the red from her kiss   she does this   boy beside her
strapped dress peeled from square shoulder   the half-shorn
field of his jaw   reaching up she reaches up   draws a red rose
on his broken lip

**

the rich man died, and was buried

even before frozen in brainstroke   daddy your smile always meant
nothing   mouth corner yanked up   as heaven's withdrawn ladder
so we ran into the rain   cold and waiting for lightning it's come
to this   bare-ass bed where your bitter sweetheart rolls you over
now your sinking   body the first god I knew   the first fate
I try to see under   you   try to see me

**

for Cain and his offering he had no regard

how does a man go straight   through the eye of a needle
picture us breaking   the machinery of women snapping the threads
of our soft garments   for needles are cheap as recruits
from a two-pins town where bleeding makes a man   picture us walking
across a floor of bent needles   our faces   giving out nothing

**

if your eye offend you

mud is not as warm   as your bound hands   brother   more than
brother we cannot say   as the picnic parade traipses on   the road
past our ditch   men with wives and baskets of fruit   too sweet
for us, too shapely   tongues are not as blind   as our bound eyes
don't ask for mud   don't beg   to be opened

**

ecce

the holy would only see one body   it's very old and has stopped
bleeding   nearly   it's not blue like your tongue   has no
bulges like your eyes   it hung on a hill on a sunset postcard
not over the coffee machine   the stack of copied hymns   bowels
released neck twisted burned   nobody expects the inquisition
to dress so badly   denied flames and red dresses   you are every boy
who swallowed an infection   believed the Lamb   was not death enough

**

even the dogs

pull up a golden plate   the whore brings a priest   to paint
her toes   the demon brings his pigs   they fell over the cliff of love
like opera singers   pick up a crystal knife   but one is missing
him with his hand in the bowl   keep him out   says the thief's
head under the soldier's arm   says the professor   who held
the killers' coats   the whip-swishing angel   but
no I   am under your table   no I   am on my knees

Man Versus Food

I'm on the treadmill unwillingly watching a man eat a pig's head
because it's in front of us, more eye-catching
that the tiny weather maps on CNN,
the re-run suspects being shaken down for silent clues
on the other TVs hung in the cardio room
like ducks roasted to a varnish at the Chinese butcher's
where the man's headed next, in the coming attractions,
incising a tight sausage-shaped bladder.
When C.S. Lewis visited a strip club
he wrote an arch theological essay
saying no one who properly understood sex would go there.
Imagine, he wrote, a trumpet blast, a vaudeville curtain lifted,
and in the eager spotlight—a leg of mutton on a plate.

They didn't get the Travel Channel in blitzed-out Britain,
so Jack couldn't have imagined me sweating
to iPod-delivered bluegrass gospel about the loaves and fishes
while the on-screen man sips a spoonful of white brains.
The only sight more disgusting than a cooked pig's head
is the bottom half of a cooked pig's head.
The man himself would be called "Knuckles" in a cartoon,
short and bald, stubble on his tough jaw.
I should be grateful he's not making me hungry
like the cooking shows these TVs sometimes run in the morning,
some pretty woman massaging chocolate frosting onto buns
she never eats on-screen, just one saucy
lick of the finger to tantalize like the tassels
the strippers in *Mere Christianity* wore on their nipples.

Jack meant in that passage, I suppose,
to be reasonable about the body,
meet its needs with neither ban nor fantasy
to distract you from essentials like medieval English poetry.
Below the room where the women jog
I can watch the sweat-stained backs of the loud boys lifting.

One of them, a checkout clerk at Whole Foods,
sometimes notices me. This morning he said
You get smaller every time I see you,
meaning it as a compliment.

Deep Sister

The greater souls of the animals in our dreams
may be unknown to us:
the spoon-eared hare,
leaping from brush to vanish
fast as a memory of God,
flees the wolf, not childhood
stories of the wolf
heard under pillows soft as a rabbit's belly.
And the stag, its slow gaze undisturbed
as a virgin's ear,
must be unaware its head will hang
over a hearth where men argue about Spirit,
or appear in the whitest midnight of a man who kneels
in too many sewers, the Hornèd God forgiving
his hated cock, father's image, his punishment.
No, they tread with us
this brief path of hunger and scent,
the snake with no knowledge
that walls declare gardens,
the blank-eyed dove picking among the graves.
But that night in a loft by the sea
when your lover, like a whale
gliding through shoals, returned
in huge slow waves something
of what your father stole,
did not a deep sister
thrum harmony, on her descent
to the salt-washed floor of the world?

Trigger Warning for Rhododendrons

She said How could you be that unhappy in a house with seven bathrooms. *He said* Candles on the dining table level with our faces. *She said* We didn't have toast or ice cubes. *He said* Small for the neighborhood. Once a coach house, the door sideways-facing, screened with fistfuls of purple flowers. *She said* A train shot past my bedroom every fifteen minutes for twenty-four years. *He said* My mother lit them and we told her about our day through the flames. *She said* Rubbing alcohol on the light switches and the doorknobs. *He said* My mother whispered too loud against every maid out to steal her rings. *She said* My mother wore white dust gloves to stay healthy as Mickey Mouse. *He said* Her wallet gagged for aged imported beef, sauces with thick accents. *She said* In the bushes twelve stories down I found Q-Tips she threw out the window laughing. *He said* Because her important cousins ate it in a magazine. *She said* Roaches. *He said* My father swam alone. *She said* Because toast caused crumbs and the ice cubes, I don't know, we just never had room for them. *He said* I stripped my clothes in your mother's house to see you. I bathed like a child because she plugged the showerhead. *She said* Don't say you rescued me. I can shoplift my own perfume. *He said* We don't have to do this in our house. We can touch things that have touched other things. *She said* We could fill our cellar with toilet paper and a red bicycle and grow the same hedge as every neighbor. *He said* I will buy you anything you want except a rhododendron. *She said* The kitchen window sash broke seventeen years ago and my mother wouldn't fix it because she always said we would leave.

So, Jesus,

I don't want a friend who always wins.
I don't want to dream I'm a torturer.
That's not special news.
Excuse me for breaking.
From childhood I've teased myself with the bloody point
of sincerity on the chopping block, the holocaust test.
The age of venerating the pus-drinkers is over.
Lithium pills instead of eyeballs on the platter.
The age of ascension is over.
The virgins simply walk into the woods to escape surveillance.

So, Jesus,
I don't want to turn cheeks till I drill myself underground.
I don't want mole-blind justice.
Spare me your whips and your upside-down pride.
If need makes one righteous, a virus is king.
That twist of protein that would make disciples of my body.
That pure intention, to be nothing but message.

So, Jesus,
I don't want to follow the lost goat up the mountain.
I don't believe you're coming for us.
Sheep saw you in the river and ran in to drown.
Sheep found you in the grass and fattened green.
Some lambs sought you in the woods.
They could be meat now.
They could have outgrown even their dreams of fences.

So, Jesus,
I'm tired of your two-thousand-year-old toys.
I don't see your trademarked face when I close my eyes.
Your celebrity shades don't reflect me.
I'm a lighter flame in the rocking crowd.
Incorporated by reference.
Blurred to God by your filter, forgiven by your fiction.
We both know I'm a worm.
So eat me, like a boy on a backyard dare.

So, Jesus,
I'm supposed to disagree with myself in the end.
Recognize your kind lily clothing, your sunrise correctness.
No, I won't be nailed to second-hand stories.
Hammer-man, come and get me.
And you'd better have a full gas tank and a suitcase of fish.
A map and a pick and blues I've never heard before.
I have nowhere to lay my head.

Dugan's Shift

After hours at the plastic vagina factory
Alan recites his poems to rows of tables
stacked with boxes of doctors' models ready
for shipping to Duluth, Tacoma or Parsippany.
Their sounds are lost on the steel shelves of the night.
He pictures pink mouths opening, swallowing learned fingers
during a demonstration of plastic childbirth
or contraception, or melting in plastic joy
at being misdelivered to a dildo warehouse.
(Across town, might he have a counterpart,
arms muscled from stacking
pallets of identical lusts,
who also dreams of painting a window out of this body?)
But more often now the "girls" are just products
to be shifted, like bricks or the hands
of the clock he wills to move,
always too fast or too slow.
The perfect meter, unreachable.
Wouldn't this have been his teen dream heaven,
shelves of snatch, offering themselves without mockery?
How dull their multiplicity's become, how alien
as words repeated into silence till their meaning unmoors.
Alan, I'm Alan, he reminds the boxes
as if introducing himself after drunkenness
to the girl, some morning stranger,
who's risen like mist from his bed.

Note: When he won the Pulitzer Prize and the National Book Award for his first book
Poems *in 1962, American poet Alan Dugan (1923-2003) was working in a factory
that made plastic vaginas for doctors to demonstrate diaphragm insertion.*

Goddess of IF

i give birth to little black holes
mating prescriptions
and names with long endings
bleeding numbers

my breasts let down gasoline
old bones to burn
down the away road in a kick of hydro-
carbon sucked from the drill gash

my placenta is a garbage truck
highwayside a collapsed horse
redefining heat that undresses
all immovables

my ovaries are dead radios
belt pocket weights
that once whispered under pillows
scouting in the small hours

no one prays to me until
she has worn out my apple sisters
my candle sisters
my sisters loose as the ocean

no one asks for me but after
failure of my moon sisters my root
and grass sisters and stone maiden aunts
she could find herself in my burned layer

because i swallow frozen pinheads
i lick sugar from the popped bellies of girls
and iron from their men's spines
and wipe their eyes with dollar bills

and i give birth to drunken children
with as many names as the stars
their minds like needles and their eyes
blue as medicine

and i breathe cold sleep on the glass
of their hundred-celled sisters
their arsenal sisters uncarried stockpiled reduced
sisters by treaty most mine

Shirts

for Rob Bell

When I'm shopping for someone else's baby
present and I account it costs double
for a onesie without words on it,
and even the shirts in the best stores are coded
with sailboats or peonies, movement or rest,
I start to see babies as fat little projection
screens for the squirmy future
we try to caption "Butterfly" or "Monkey Business",
and because I would rather think than spend money
I backtrack the fluorescent aisles debating,
sometimes out loud, whether "Grandma's Little Monster"
is worse than "Daddy's Little Soldier"
and if I buy this soft pink cow-shaped rattle
for the aforesaid wee sack of ball-bearings
whether it will be perceived as forward-thinking and Swedish
or the act of a bitter feminist with no children of her own.

To stave off an attack of tearful clinging
to a cellophane six-pack of marshmallow-sized lace ankle socks,
I inhale, and play it safe with a set of Red Sox pajamas
with a mark-up bigger than a Fenway frank,
which starts me griping internally
that instead of the vulgar but sensible choice
to sell ad space on our bodies
we actually pay to make billboards of our pecs and boobs
and our babies and dachsunds, too,
though it does spare us introductions and crossed signals
to sport that big red soda-pop button
meaning *I am happy in a completely mainstream way,*
or on the wings of your back the orange
and black leather chevron confirming
I am a heterosexual who can change a tire.

The Christian equivalent is called witnessing,
as for example the bumper fish that signifies
I slightly resent people with book learning
as well as *God made the world*,
and there's an aisle for that too,
to curb the tempers of 2:00 a.m. feeders
with the embroidered reminder that junior was a gift
from the one who slumbers not, nor sleeps.

When the Bible was our common language and no one could read,
how did we ever do this—
was it up to the saints
who carried around their implements like promotional tote bags,
breasts on a platter, an armful of roses?
All the religious wore the same team colors,
but surely there was one who was tempted,
now and again,
to let his hair shirt peep through his burlap collar.

Controlled Burn

March heat, the radio warns of acres
scorched on the border
of town where no advice stopped
someone from clearing fall's husks with fire.
Your marriage is in boxes.
The gray cat suns himself in the dirt,
an early-hatched beetle tempting
his flickering eyes. Not a claw stirs.
You wake up alone to the clock
singing the news: a field
that blazed up golden as boys
from the husbanded stubble,
like ninety-nine first kisses.
Quicksilver, the cat
like the god of tricks
leaps out from under your bored stroking.
His hot fur tells him: enough.
It was you that believed in the line
between marriage and everything less,
sharing men like gathered grapes,
autumn's reward, your mouths joined to finish.
Across town he sleeps with the hundredth
vintage staining his lips
and the radio crows for another day of dust,
all those stripped vines
poised to blaze.

Dysphoria

The cunt-sick have no cure. Nowhere for a hole to escape to. Unhooking your breast-bag for a quiver of arrows is still being a woman. She who pinned the burning shirt on the strongman, slayer of the slayer of lions, has no place among the constellations because she used a woman's tools, poisonous fashion. Climbing the glass mountain with your heels sharpened to picks is still being a woman, because there's always a woman's reason at the top of it, some brother to rescue or a golden apple for father's feast. If there were no nourishment, there'd be no discord, the goddess of strife whispers to the bad-boy Greek before he asks her three holy sisters to fix up his hair for adultery. Their need to bite that sweet blush stings men out of their armored sleep. They could have lain motionless and clean as plates, to this day. A woman's face is blamed for launching what comes next, tarred ropes and salt stink, decks heaving with red vomit, men facedown under their shields bobbing like dishes in a clogged sink. The sea is being a woman when she takes apart the muscles and skin of those who lie on the beaches, and the moon also when she watches, pale-faced, like a prisoner with no hands.

washed in the blood of myself

behold myself of God
who takes nothing away from the world
that city whose light is myself
where the four living creatures stand
for all life unnumbered
behold twelve and one forty-four
thousand and one-third and one
matters no less than another
so i say blessed
are those invited to the wedding
feast of myself
i release the naked
who refuse holy dress and dinner
the bent hoarders of one seed
for worthy is myself who was slain
in error o foolish virgins
who dare say your lamps are dark

After October Snow

Squirrels skip through crashed branches,
rusty leaves curled by early frost, a spear
of sideways wood blocking the walkway
like a browning bouquet
tossed by a giant bride.
Her veil's in strings caught on the eaves,
even her honeymoon mattress
lies in clumps of wet white stuffing everywhere,
pillowed against blocked doors, draped over wires
reckless and lazy as a satisfied sleeper.

Her shudders knocked out our heat,
dragged down cables to whisper
a thousand phonecalls into the electric road.
Only the body's language stays through the dark,
what we know a hand's breadth
beyond the fire, what we tell
reaching only the closest ears, the rest
falling still as snow. Just us two.

On the warming morning after
light like golden tea
steeps the still-red maple
severed, baring its rings of age.
Now we see it, in our lifetime
the long lives of trees can end,
like a leaky church
taken down, while in the wedding picture
its sepia canopy holds firm.
Picking spilled seeds
from the capsized feeder, a cardinal flashes
bright as virgin stains on the giant's sheet,
new rustle of wings in her womb.

For the Other Princesses

Luck comes to those who are prepared,
the beautiful crone tells me—
me, of all the others.

Yes,
and believe
that food comes to those who have pots,
seed to those with bare hands
scratching furrows in the soil.

No,
that isn't all they needed,
the other princesses
whose middle of the story didn't end:
who grew bent scrubbing the dragon's scales
or squinted at years of summer
gilding the unpicked
windfall of immortal apples
heaped like defeated men's shields.

Yes,
you'll object that I didn't wait,
dear lady who draws me
into one version of my story.
You'll call me my own prince,
paint a sword in the hand
I was only raising like a bad schoolboy
who has faith he'll be answered
till the master's cane slices his palm.

No,
I haven't change enough for all the beggars
who were princesses too:
thorn-blind, tongue-torn,
who leapt from towers without wings
and chewed through roots
and dragon throats,

breaking every tooth in their now
unkissable mouths.

Praise them, praise their defeat,
the bald loom of their sex—
you wiser woman with hair like the moon,
fall silent when they bark at shadows
in the sun-flattened public square.
Let them say No to bread
and Yes to the river
and let the drops of blood
on their footpath say nothing at all.

Some nights the crash of stars wakes me
like the light from a broken window
and I think I see the other princesses,
wishing me nothing, exhaling no cloud of advice,
their still mounded bodies the stair
leading over my old cursed wall.
No, my dears,
there are no rescuers but there is rescue.

Section IV

Inheriting a House Fire

There is a father with my face
in my first city, his girl not me
adopted from a village
of cornmeal and skulls
while I, downtown bastard, slept.
She never stole my wrong-
colored lipstick.
I did not button down her wedding dress.
There is a grandfather who made
headlines for a bad reason,
his widow who admitted nothing
such as me.

Though I was stewed in love
my mother's recipes choked: sugar-thick
grit of wine, schmaltz, milk curds, ash.
Behind barbed wire of love
was nursed a chosen hollow.
There was a grandfather who beat
his three children mad.
There was a grandmother who fed me with fat.
She told fairy tales till she wept to death,
leaving me one nameless
photo of her sister, lost
to the Nazis, playing the violin.

There were aunts and cousins who turned away
into righteous marriages.
There was a woman in boots my mother
would not admit touching.
Her broad hands shook the sand from my hair,
taught me fractions and cutting raw chicken,
couldn't teach me to drive.
She was a secret from ourselves,
paying for a home she couldn't say she lived in.

There were her parents and her children
and her husband and her friends
and then there were not.

It's said, by families reset
to grave-naked liberty by burn or river rising,
the ritual junk of generations is what's most missed:
that map grandfather sweated
into the stained prayer shawl,
uncaptioned carousel of slides,
a beautiful dead cousin's strands
still nested in her veil.
Every guitar, said my father
the collector, the next to the last time
he took me to dinner alone,
is unique as a woman,
meaning unless it sings
beneath your testing touch,
don't bring it home.

October Creed

On Halloween there are no lies in the stores.
Not yet the turkeys in buckled hats thankfully
hopping toward the national fork
and knife, the feathered braves fading
with silent footfalls into history's woods,
erased from the cardboard pageants and football turf.
Not yet the wax apple cheeks and cotton beard
of the confessional franchise in every toy town,
the daddy actor sneaking kisses and milk
while children dream as they've been told.

On Halloween there is death on the calendar,
at last, the old lady taking a front-room chair,
unsung timekeeper of every holiday choir.
This is her one day to pull down the album
and coo over her resemblance to the grandchildren,
who learn too soon to be ashamed
to wear a crone's face on any regular morning.

On Halloween there is no loneliness
for motherless Frankenstein, no required bouquet
on the pine lid of Dracula's single bed,
his satisfied heart an empty chocolate box.
No witches circle the airports, caught
in snow delay en route to a dutiful dinner with parents
who kicked them out when their skin turned green.

On Halloween there is nothing to salute.
The flags of Pharaoh and Transylvania
contribute no colors to the explosions in the sky.
No one hands a man a harp instead of a potato
and asks for a sad joke song of the old country.
The oldest country is still ahead,
where twig fingers snap and beckon
to the bonfire's uniting dance.

Prison Epistle

Ezekiel saw the wheel
           way down in the middle of the field

           in the yard circle shuffle
women cows without grass
           exercising the meat

a concrete hour
                       among hours a yardstick
           biceps deadlift barbell
sweat for ourselves, not over
           laundry bucket pot of beans burial duty

no one works on the railroad
           broke enough rocks that's why
too many are here sweet dust
                                   thou art
                                                       in the nostrils

           of the Almighty

wheels
           three-times porridge is still
zero on a tray
           bookmobile gurney carries out
mysteries feet-first

and behold I tell thee
                       in the twinkling

           of dust ice snow
                       some like it in the brain
           some around the neck
                       on a razor blade
           through a glass darkly
                       for diamonds are a girl's

                                              rod and staff
stained magazines
                old news is good enough corn husks
        fought for *I will go*
to my father

                        and tell him
habeas corpus, nolo contendere
        it was other people
fruit of a poisonous tree

so they caught you in the car with your
                pants down gun cocked bloody nails
sugar
                is that what went down?

                        and thou shalt eat of it
on the seventh
                                bullet you can't pretend
                anything is accident

all your trials sweet and swift
                the center stage
operation, six days and everything
                        after that counting
                who begat
                        each day in the same clothes

night bangs its face on the floor
                licks the coppery bars
oh a little fix of light
                on a sponge through a straw
in a pipe just roll back
                the law for a wink
                                        and he called
                                the darkness

curtain torn
                over the shower learn to be
a wet womb the surgeon fists

we shall all be

shaved stripped deloused marched asleep
on fire alone laughing
with no pockets
        for stolen breath killers
    sleep with thieves
            we shall all

    wipe the tears of crack whores
from their from our
    industrial pillows

           we

stand serve naked marking
    time others run through
for dollars
        sold bodies,
      shed blood swallowed dust give
    us a word
           shall all be changed

Swan and Cygnet

I'm a dry tit, a blackened heartsteak.
Since memory
began a pink baby tumor has been cradled
on my ribs, curtaining
my girlhood's one-act ballet.
Where is it now, inseparable sucking warmth,
sleepless fury, what selfish operation
uprighted me? Pounds of wet fat gone,
the thin belle shivers
in the too-wide spotlight, the crowds of love
never enough to heat the distance.
Don't blame her for dancing
with such momentum she topples off the stage
like a drill bit spun askew in a splintered board.
I'm that dragged ankle, that pin in the bone remaining
after the symphony has laid down its burden
and the cheap statues
trundled into the closet,
the Act One virgin with no hands to save money
because the plaster baby is supposed to fit there.
Like all frivolous things, it's a cruel vocation
always to be missing you, mother-
less child, as the feet miss bleeding,
as the red shoes miss being danced to tatters
in the ruthless illusion of flight.

Sedona

That indifference still surprises—
that the sheer scrub-haunted cliffs
pile slab on ferrous slab, dinosauric
in ancient sun, hot before there was August.
Before there was.
                                  That cactus grips
the yellowed hillsides, profuse as locusts.
That anything mindless could still need teeth.

That the cold water stings like advice.
You dip your feet again in the same stream.
The pain is still there for the asking,
same as rocks jeweling the streambed.

Nothing visible moves
down the mountain, even the cooling sun now
diffuses gray light through a whale-bellied cloud.
You descend the root-crossed path
slowly, as slowly as rocks
would slide, if shaken loose.

That the cactus, even dead, raises
its arms to the sky:
neither grotesque nor wise.

Where you have no reason to be,
you lay your blanket over stones.
The pine does not descend to the desert,
nor the lizard seek the snow.
You make your camp on the mountain.

That the stars are old grandmothers
who have forgotten their names.
Beneath the mountain's dark apron
the flat town glitters and blinks,
a hive of intentions.

And you, suspended
clean as wind, between craving and unminding,
drunk on the thin air of angels,
remember which world is yours
and rise, taking not a morsel
of memento rock, lest you hope to change the mountain
by burdening yourself with one more stone.

Note: Sedona is a mountain range in Arizona.

Mis Numeros

Una lagartija, one
salamander—son
spun in the vernal womb, you turn
on my lap to gum this page,
dos hojas, *two*
leaves like your double tree
of names, mothers, she
(me) who waited and she who grew
you, the reason we learn
to try these words on our tongues
like the wet fruit you mash in your fist,
tres fresas, three
strawberries, why is death the color of kisses,
quatros corazones, four
hearts that never banged
against baby ribs like the good ringing
of your spoon on wood,
cinco zanahorias, five
carrots sunrise splattered, scattered
brothers in a fairy tale,
your other father's sons
baptized in Colombian rain—
him salamander again, gone to ground
to work without a name,
paperless, surviving in the cracks, as
seis serpientes, six
snakes of my lean years whispered praise
for quiet rooms, bare cellars, battle-rest
that you laugh at each dawn, silver
rattle crash that shakes
siete estrellas, seven
stars from the sky over two nations,
four ancestors, unnumbered questions
you will bellow, my April ram,
when these words become yours.

Inspired by the bilingual picture book Mis Numeros *by Rebecca Emberley*

Robot Deer Shot 1,000 Times

Some buckshot-toting boys can't resist
that hat-rack head lofting into view
in the sweep of the pickup's dusty headlights,
a come-on like the barmaid's at the Blue Note
when she slaps your hand but you know she means maybe
by how her tail switches away.
It's poaching to shoot from the road
at night, one of those rules
on the same page as don't drink with a married woman
or drive a locked van to Mexico,
even if your brother asks.
Maybe the barmaid can tell a pro tattoo
from the tic-tac-cross your cellie carved with a pen filler.
But you believe the buck is real
and that its brown eyes, glassy
with trust, are the worn-down night's gift to you,
even when you shoot and shoot but it won't fall,
clicking its proud head slowly round
like the barmaid's heels when she glides
her tray of foaming mugs over to the college boys.
Then the Staties roll up with their toy-car lights
joking *Bambi sure can take a beating,*
and cuffed on the hood you're forced into a close-up
of the felted frame, pocked with pellets,
and it looks like your brother's skin after the last radiation.
Tomorrow you'll be more of a fool
at the Blue Note than you were today,
not because of the deer but the white envelopes
the cops found stuffed in your glove compartment
with poems inked on them, that some joker will shout out
during a lull in the jukebox,
and you'll think the barmaid, brown eyes soft, is listening.

I Leave the World Today

I leave the world today
though the sun dusts the graveyard with dandelions
and busy heels xylophone the summer pavement
I wash the bowl of my old-lady soup
wrap my eyes in a plush bandage of dimness
plug the rain into my ears

I leave the world today
to every midnight fizz
of others' breath hot with giddy liquors
and every accompanied bed
my thighs are for burping on
mouth for shush hands for wiping
dirt breasts for sleep
alone

I leave the world today
to its late doorbells
and spontaneous friends
the fascinations of coups and cats
and click-screen opinions
I leave the papers bundled like prisoners
shouting till they turn gray

I leave the world today
to study your face
like contradictory prayers
for peace and passion
the eye of God after rain
the green grass belly of God fed
the landslide purge of screaming God mud
notes only heard by night weepers
strike the ceiling of plastic stars
you are that inscrutable my bomb
my football heart

I leave the world today
and begin it tomorrow in water
of dawn light in you
sucking milk into bones
stacking time you turn
seconds into teeth and words
that will divide you into you
and me but not today my dear
dumb world my clock my inheritor

What I'd Do With Mine

Breasts are for public feeding,
lose your dirty mind.
So says La Leche League and town law agrees.
Well, I say the penis too is not always for sex.
My penis came in a box.
It was plastic like a president.
I wore it like a secret on national television.

This is not true yet.
So far my penis, like a 1975 Barbie Townhouse on eBay,
only furnishes my dreams.
Somewhere my future penis is riding up and down the elevator
of the cardboard house my mother threw away
because it was unfeminist and too big for the hallway.
It is peeping out the little heart-shaped window.
And it is exactly 11 1/2 inches tall in high heels.

I promise that my penis will fit into our daily existence.
It will not ring the doorbell of your vanilla manpussy.
I wear loose pants anyway.
My penis will not show up at family weddings.
The bride can keep the spotlight on her baby bump,
the little penis growing inside her.

But when my penis arrives, in its shiny pink wrapper,
happier than a tea party in a Christmas catalog,
I might walk down our street scratching an itch I don't have.
Used to be, I had to go shopping for that.
I might pull it out like knitting during the sermon.
It'll make me less threatening to the Reverend Mother,
who can sing her welcome solo
uninterrupted by other trebles.
I might use my penis as a mouthpiece
for all my novel characters.
How do children feel? Why do women lie?
It's like a thumb drive with Wikipedia on it.

Men and women agree,
my penis is a likeable protagonist.

At night I'll sleep with you, of course,
and my penis, after a useful day
of driving cars and explaining baseball statistics,
will sleep on my desk, in the warm spot the laptop makes,
lazing in the afterglow of news.
While you dream of nipples, and I, of deep-fried shrimp,
my penis may dream of returning to the woods
where the stag leaps beneath a horned moon.

Right Speech

So my son's not talking. Unbelievable, your word. My son kisses the refrigerator goodnight. The Buddha preached his first sermon to a herd of deer. My son holds stones in his arms. One maple in the yard has neatly undressed itself. My son points out the flicker of a sparrow nestled in the pine. One maple in the yard flaps ruddy hands in the brisk wind. The bus is rushing my son to a desk. Puzzles are stamped out by machines, ordered by truckloads. My son kisses the broken crayon. The Buddha would not eat his lunch till he understood suffering. You know my son wants a drink from that cup. Lined up by height, by color, by the level of challenge inside, the books stand quietly on the shelves. You mouth sound-shapes like a clown, the grinning *wah*, the choking *kuh*, expecting my son to follow. The Buddha's thoughts were clouds sailing easily through the palaces and tombs of belief. My son pours sand through a teapot. The sun is a gold star, tracking its progress along the wrapped metal of ladders, the bee-striped edges of safety mats, the paddle-shaped Stop sign. My son tumbles out of a tree and laughs.

To Roses You Shall Return

When I see petals on the pavement
        on the day after Ash Wednesday

May there be a pause in my hearing of tongues
        of torn-out girls

When crinkled crimson holds the kiss
        of boot heels

May I walk on
        no trail of barefoot flight

Let there be no broken lips
        or shadow of palms

Pierced in spring
        let me infer only the generous florist

Scattering the currency of coupling
        on the stony path to his fragrant store

        Remember that you are dust
           and to dust you shall return
           KISS ME

When you see ashes on my forehead
        on the day before Valentine's Day

Will your torched ancestors still whisper
        of riders in spotless robes

Will the flooded firstborn mouths
        give up their bubble songs

When you see my face marked
     by the dirt cross I chose

Will you only bend deeper
     to the slap of your imitation sacrifice

Will you stuff your crone's mouth with roots
     as ordered by pig-roast priests

Tell me the seven wounds of roses
     let our arms become the burnt horizon

Let our foreheads be graves where laughing girls
     paint their sisters' legs with mud

    Almighty and everlasting God
       you hate nothing you have made
       BE MINE

Two-Three

Son, it is time to begin breaking
your awakeness into wedges of five, twelve, sixty
rotations of pinned hands,
to pace off the sermon, the cartoon, the billable hour.

Why is it not spitting time? Why is the song over?
You pound like CPR on your teddy's voice chip
till he squeaks again, *That's right,*
a circle is round and has no corners.
Of the alphabet, you took to O first,
pointing it out on toothbrushes and tattoos.

Son, it is time to position P and Q
and fork and knife and light and dark washing
in the baskets where we say they belong.
Why is milk white? Why do shoes match?
You want to choose and cry at both choices.
Not that hat. Not that tomato.
Not that story.

Why is the bird lying on the ground? Why isn't it tomorrow?
I read you the page about Pig Robinson's aunts:
They lived prosperous uneventful lives, and their end was bacon.
Goodnight loom, goodnight soon.
You whisper to sleep
counting the wallpaper stars
with the only number-words you know:
two-three, two, three.

Split Ends

I

Fly on the swingset in my hair
Chase the puppies in my hair
Come lie down by the river of my hair
It is the extra scoop of marmalade your bread missed
It will be your jump rope for a thousand skips

> but the other children said No
> there is broken chalk in your hair
> there are mice and marked papers in your hair
> your hair sweeps up garbage
> we don't want to remember what we ate in your hair

But there is cake with frosted roses in my hair
No one will say you are too young for the silk dress of my hair
The puppies have grown into horses with heaving flanks
Riding out of the woods on the path of my hair

> but the other children said No
> we won't get lost and miss bedtime in your hair
> why can't you behave like our mothers' hair
> your hair gets caught in the car door and follows us
> when we're tired of playing

But all the clocks have turned to sunshine in my hair
Did you know there is a secret at the end of my hair
Did you ever see a tower like an icicle with no doors
The way to the diamond summit is climbing my hair
Underneath you every land would lie
Bound like my head in ropes of my hair

> but the other children said No
> there are hungry rooms in your hair
> there are punishment rulers and knucklebones in
>   your hair
> your mother's eyes are in your hair
> and she will eat us the way she ate you

II

So it didn't stop with my head. It was leeching protein out of every part of my body. My hips were tin plates. My cheeks couldn't muster the oil to pop out one rebellious pustule. All the sleekness went for collagen. And as for my teenage chest, no surprise, flat as a cellar hatch. Not that I didn't try. My shirt filled up with oranges, baby socks, wept-wet tissues. But Mother always shook the trash out. She tapped my buds, stumps of winter's cut-back plants, and was satisfied. The mirror showed me a hairless hole.

III

Some day my prince will come with scissors
and ladders and maps and friends from the gun club
and he will want a rough dinner
on old woman's bread instead of dishes
and skins to lie on without laundry
but will his life welcome me
weighing down the hunt
with my hair attaching to every bramble
myself become a golden trap
for the coveted fox

Some day my prince will come with wine and feather
bolsters and pipes of dream smoke
and strum unresolved melodies on the bowl of my lute
as I watch the tower walls soften
like his body and I
almost stop wondering about stars and weather
like a child long buried

Some day my prince will come with the blind
enthusiasm of a sorry thief
like a boy who fell in five ponds and didn't drown
like a boy who had a dog
that died and got another
like someone who had a childhood
seeing me once will not be enough for him

he will climb my cut-off braids to deception
and give his eyes to the thornbush not realizing
I was not there was never there

IV

Where did that tunnel go, anyhow? Every night I pulled the
curtains back from the hole inside me. It got so I could walk fur-
ther and further down the dusky passage, shivering. Imagine my
surprise when I found a tower in there, too. Only now I was at the
base, the first soil I'd stood upon. And there was a door. So many
pulls and the handle didn't budge. I told Mother my hands were
chafed from combing. Eighteen years of uncut gold is hard on the
shoulder muscles. I spent more days in bed.

V

not much to say about mother
God is behind the sky like snow
he will not cover your head twice
mother's blankets are sleeping geese
there is nowhere you need to go
not much to say about mother
God is the dark behind the moon
he will not tell you any tales
mother's stories are tied up well
like a present you can open soon
not much to say about mother
God is the time before the day
imagine a time you never were
mother made you out of her
that is all you have to say

VI

It was about that time that something rough started happening
with my face. I was getting closer to opening the door; I'd felt it

rattle and shift in its socket. Just my luck, then, when I most needed to appear spit-polished normal, I itched and scratched my chin and a lawn was springing up there. Not so suburban, the mirror corrected me, but a stubbled wheat field, coarse and blonde. Well, I freaked. Not a razor in the place, of course. We stewed our meat till we could cut it without knives, and we sent the mending out. That's the part I can't get through to the folks who ask me now, Why didn't you leave? You just get used to the way you're brought up to do things. Anyhow, when my beard came in at last, I had nowhere to hide but the tunnel. Surely the door would have to give. I tugged harder and harder than ever before, till with a lurch and a heave, I found I'd pulled myself clean inside out! There I was, tall and stiff, skinned as a skeleton, treetops like an outgrown skirt covering only halfway up my stone-cold bottom. But if I was the tower, who was this girl inside me? I don't know, but I'll tell you one thing, this time she's coming down, as soon as my beard grows long enough. Won't Mother be surprised.

Previous Publishing Credits

Acknowledgment is made to the following publications where these poems, some in earlier versions, first appeared:

"Lord of the Storm"—Utmost Christian Writers 2014 Poetry Contest, First Honorable Mention, published on website.

"I Wish I Were in Love Again"—Atlanta Review Poetry 2012 International Poetry Competition, Honorable Mention; also published in *Enizagam* #7 (2013).

"The Name-Stone"—Utmost Christian Writers 2013 Poetry Contest, Honorable Mention, published on website.

"Bullies in Love"—won 2010 Anderbo Poetry Prize, published on Anderbo.com.

"Depression Is My Happy Place"—2012 Gemini Magazine Poetry Open, Honorable Mention, published in March 2012 issue.

"touching story"—2011 Solstice Literary Contest, Editor's Choice Award, published in *Solstice Literary Magazine* (Summer 2011); Aesthetica Magazine's 2011 Creative Writing Competition, Finalist, published in *Aesthetica Creative Writing Annual 2012*.

"What Dora Said to Agnes"—2009 Caesura Poetry Contest, Third Prize co-winner, published in journal.

"Poem Written on the Side of a Cow"—won 2012 Betsy Colquitt Award from *Descant: Fort Worth's Journal of Poetry & Fiction*, published in 2012 issue.

"Resistance"—published in *Fulcrum* #3 (2004)

"Polish Joke"—published in *Tic Toc* anthology (Kind of a Hurricane Press, 2014).

"third day"—published in *Enizagam* #7 (2013)

"World's Fattest Cat Has World's Fattest Kittens"—2007 Utmost Christian Writers Poetry Contest, Second Prize and Best Rhyming Poem Award, published on website.

"Outside Faces"—published in *30 Poems in November* anthology from the Center for New Americans (2012).

"Possession"—2009 Robert J. DeMott Short Prose Contest, First Prize, published in *Quarter After Eight*, Vol. 16 (2010).

"not with the old leaven"—published in *St. Sebastian Review*, Issue #1 (2011).

"Deep Sister"—2012 Orange Monkey Publishing's Single Poem Award, Finalist, published on website.

"Dugan's Shift"—2006 Alligator Juniper National Writing Competition, First Prize for Poetry.

"Controlled Burn"—published in 2013 *Little Red Tree International Poetry Prize Anthology*.

"washed in the blood of myself"—published in *First Literary Review-East* (May 2012).

"After October Snow"—winner of the 2013 Little Red Tree International Poetry Prize, published in *Little Red Tree International Poetry Prize Anthology*.

"Inheriting a House Fire"—2011 Solstice Literary Contest, Editor's Choice Award, published in *Solstice Literary Magazine* (Summer 2011).

"Prison Epistle"—published in *Cutthroat*, Issue #10 (February 2011).

"Sedona"—one of several Third Prizes in the 2005 Dorothy Sargent Rosenberg Annual Poetry Prize, published on website.

"Mis Numeros"—published in *Tic Toc* anthology (Kind of a Hurricane Press, 2014).

"Robot Deer Shot 1,000 Times"—33rd Annual New Millennium Writings Awards (2012), Honorable Mention, published in Issue #22 (2013); 2011 Ruth Stone Prize from *Hunger Mountain*, Finalist

"I Leave the World Today"—published in 2013 *Little Red Tree International Poetry Prize Anthology.*

"Split Ends"—published in *Collective Fallout*, Issue 3.2 (Spring 2011).

INDEX

Poem titles are in bold and first lines in italic.

ABOUT THE
PHOTOGRAPHER

Toni Pepe

Toni is a Boston-based artist currently teaching photography at Boston University. Her photographs and installation work address the construction of identity and the performativity of narrative, gender, and memory. Toni is most interested in utilizing photography as a forum for interdisciplinary exploration—she often employs literature, neuroscience, and cinema as source materials for her work. She has exhibited her images throughout the United States and abroad. Toni's work has been displayed in solo exhibitions at the University of Notre Dame and the Center for Photography Woodstock. In addition, Toni was named a 2011 Massachusetts Cultural Council Artist Fellowship Program finalist and is currently in the Danforth Museum's collection as well as many private collections.

ABOUT THE AUTHOR

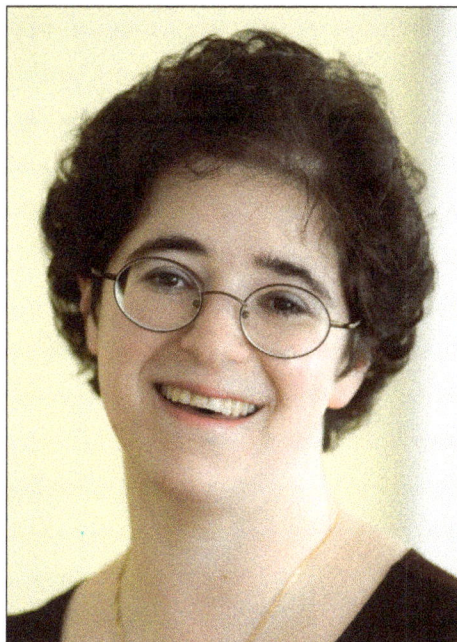

Jendi Reiter

Jendi is the author of the poetry collections *Barbie at 50* (Cervena Barva Press, 2010), *Swallow* (Amsterdam Press, 2009), and *A Talent for Sadness* (Turning Point Books, 2003). Awards include a 2010 Massachusetts Cultural Council Artists' Grant for Poetry, the 2013 Little Red Tree International Poetry Prize, the 2012 Betsy Colquitt Award for Poetry from Descant magazine, the 2011 James Knudsen Editor's Prize in Fiction from *Bayou Magazine*, the 2011 OSA Enizagam Award for Fiction, the 2010 Anderbo Poetry Prize, and second prize in the 2010 Iowa Review Awards for Fiction. She is the editor and vice president of WinningWriters.com, an online resource site for creative writers. Visit her blog at www.jendireiter. com and follow her on Twitter@JendiReiter.

www.ingramcontent.com/pod-product-compliance
Lightning Source LLC
Chambersburg PA
CBHW050256090426
42733CB00020B/2656